Roz Smith

You're Not Welsh!

Ernst Klett Verlag
Stuttgart

1. Auflage 1 7 6 5 4 3 | 2018 17 16 15 14

Alle Drucke dieser Auflage sind unverändert und können im Unterricht nebeneinander verwendet werden.

Internetadresse: www.klett.de / www.lektueren.com

Satz: Satzkasten, Stuttgart
Umschlaggestaltung: Elmar Feuerbach
Titelfoto: Mauritius / © Gutekunst
Druck: Medienhaus Plump GmbH, Rheinbreitbach
Printed in Germany.

ISBN 978-3-12-545491-0

Contents

Chapter 1

James felt the warm sunshine on his face as he lay in bed. But something was different. Then he heard the noise of a large engine outside – what could that be? It certainly wasn't Mr Armstrong's milk-van, which arrived at 7.30 every morning.

"James! James! Get up – you'll be late for school! We have to leave in twenty minutes."

Then he remembered. He wasn't in Croydon any more – he was in Llwynon, in Wales, in his new home. And the engine outside was the tractor which Mr Rees was using to carry his hay to the barn.

Oh dear! James was not happy. He had not wanted to leave Croydon and all his friends there, but his father had a new job, so now they were in Wales. It was a new start for the family – James and his mother and father.

James washed, put on his new school uniform and came downstairs for breakfast. His mother, Ann Boyd, was drinking a cup of coffee and trying to smile. But James could see that she was nervous too.

"I don't like this uniform, Mum. Why do I have to wear it?" asked James loudly.

"Well, your new head teacher told me on the telephone that a lot of children wear uniform. I think you look nice in it. Come on, hurry up! Don't forget your schoolbag."

As they walked along the village street, they saw groups of schoolchildren. They were talking and looking in the window of the village shop at the sweets on the shelves.

8 **not … any more** *nicht mehr* – 9 **Llwynon** [hluːˈwɪnɒn] – 11 **hay** *Heu* – 11 **barn** *Scheune*

"Help," thought James, "I can't understand a word they are saying ... Oh dear, it's not English – it must be Welsh."

They arrived at the school, and in the playground he saw a large sign – YSGOL LLWYNON. What did that mean? Then, in smaller letters under it, he read 'Llwynon School'.

A large man was standing at the school door, with a big smile on his face.

"*Bore da*, Mrs Boyd. Good morning. So this is James, then? Croeso! Welcome! Welcome to Llwynon School. Come with me and I'll take you to your new class."

As the children stood to one side so that they could go in, James understood that the big man must be Mr Phillips, the head teacher.

Dosbarth / Class 7, it said on the classroom door.

"*Bore da*, Mrs Evans. Good morning. This is Mrs Boyd with James. He's just arrived from Croydon."

"Good morning, Mrs Evans," said James loudly.

He smiled at everyone, but he felt uncomfortable in his new school uniform. It was a bit too big for him. Everyone was waiting for the class to begin. The other children put down their books and stared at him. James was sure they were talking about him. The best thing was to act normal and look as if it didn't matter. He watched them with a serious face as he sat down. When he looked at the door again, his mother had gone. A big, untidy boy at the front of the class stood up and started to throw his arms about wildly.

"*Sais!*" he shouted at James. "You're not Welsh!"

5 **ysgol** [ə'skɔːl] *(Welsh)* school – 10 **bore da** ['bɒrə 'dɑː] *(Welsh)* good morning – 11 **croeso** ['krɔɪsɒ] *(Welsh)* welcome – 17 **dosbarth** ['dɒsbɑːrθ] *(Welsh)* class – 21 **uncomfortable** [ʌn'kʌmfətəbl] *unbequem* – 24 **to stare** *anstarren* – 26 **as if** *als ob* – 32 **Sais** [saɪs] *(Welsh)* Englishman

Chapter 2

For the rest of the school day James tried to follow the lessons in class, but every time he gave an answer in a loud and clear voice, the other children started to laugh. His accent was *so* English.
In the end, Mrs Evans said, “Now, everyone, stop being stupid! James is working very well.”
At three thirty the bell rang, and lessons were at an end. James paid no attention to anyone. As he went down the village street, he was eating a chocolate bar that he still had in his lunch-box. But Arwel Jenkins, the boy who had shouted at him in class, came up to him.
“Give me a bit of that!” he said.
James thought that was a good idea, as he didn’t want any trouble.
“Why are you here? You’re not Welsh! You think that because you’re English and have a posh accent you’re better than us. What a joke! And you live in ‘Tŷ Ni’ – what a stupid name for a house! What was wrong with the old name? *Sais*!” And Arwel laughed again. As he left, he finished James’s chocolate.

James went home, hung his school blazer on a chair in the kitchen and threw his bag on the floor. He was glad his first day at school was finished.
“Mum,” he shouted into the living-room, “Why did you change the name of the house to ‘Tŷ Ni’? And what does it mean anyway?”
“It means ‘Our House’. Dad wanted to call it that because ‘Glanpwllafon’ was too long. We don’t

8 **to pay attention** [ə'tenʃn] **to so** hier: *jemanden/etwas beachten* – 17 **posh** *(informal) vornehm, piekfein* – 19 **Tŷ Ni** ['tiː 'niː] – 29 **Glanpwllafon** [ˌglaːnpuːhl'ɑːvɒn]

speak Welsh, but at least the name of the house is short and easy now."

Ann Boyd was feeling unhappy too. Her brother and sisters and all her friends were in South England. Neither she nor her husband Peter wanted to come to Wales. But IBM promised him a lot of money if he went to Aberaeron to help their workers there with the new computers in their offices. Peter hoped to finish the job quickly. Then the Boyd family could go back to England in a year or two.

The first week in Wales went by slowly. The children in his class laughed a lot at James, both in and out of school. He thought they were just stupid. And Mr Phillips the head teacher was wrong about the school uniform: many of the younger children in the school wore it, but in class 7 only two or three did. The others looked so old-fashioned. They had hand-knitted pullovers, traditional haircuts and old brown schoolbags. *He* looked much more modern than them! And worse than that, their accents were Welsh country accents. His *English* accent was the right way to speak!

Then the next week another new boy joined the class. Owain Hughes came from Newcastle in England, where he had lived all of his life. The children found Owain's Newcastle accent very difficult to understand, but he told them he spoke a bit of Welsh.

"My Mum lived here when she was young, and my gran always lived here. She died only last year. She knew everyone in the village," he told the pupils proudly. "I already know some Welsh and if

5 **neither** ['naɪðə]… **nor** *weder … noch* – 7 **Aberaeron** [æber'aɪrɒn] – 11 **to go by** *vergehen* – 17 **old-fashioned** *altmodisch* – 18 **hand-knitted** [hænd'nɪtɪd] *handgestrickt* – 24 **Owain** ['əʊɪn]

I go to the special classes, I'll learn a lot more, very quickly."
"Speak Welsh all the time and you'll soon make lots of friends. And don't criticise everything that's different here!" his mother told him on his first school day.
"Yes, I will, Mum. I know the kids here don't like English," Owain laughed. "Also, I'm new, so it will not be easy to make new friends here. But if I speak Welsh it will be easier."

James decided to try and make friends with Owain. "He's a new boy too, so I must be friendly and help him," he thought.
James couldn't understand why the pupils were so unfriendly to *him*. Maybe if he helped Owain in one way, Owain could do something for *him*. He could teach James a few Welsh words as an answer when they shouted at him in the playground.
James and Owain had to go to Mrs Gwen Jones's special lessons for an hour and a half each day. She had a group of learners from every class who did not know Welsh. She spoke to them slowly in Welsh and used the same phrases again and again. She also helped them with school work. She was so friendly that everyone learned Welsh quickly with her. Owain always enjoyed the lessons, but sometimes James did not. Welsh was so difficult. He quickly got fed up and could not concentrate.
Then he said loudly, "I don't want to learn Welsh. It's too difficult! What's wrong with English? Most people speak English."
Mrs Jones did not get angry easily. "Never mind, James," she said. "You'll soon learn Welsh with me.

4 **to criticise** ['krɪtɪsaiz] – 28 **to be fed up** *die Nase voll haben* – 28 **to concentrate** ['kɒnsntreɪt]

Don't worry! It will be easier in a few weeks – you'll see!"

After school one day James met Owain, who was walking home alone.
"Hello, Owain," he said. "Are you OK? I'm glad I'm not the only new boy now. Where do you live?"
"I live in 'Ynys Las' – it's the first farm round the corner here. It was my gran's. You can come up and visit me if you like."
"OK," answered James. "I'll tell my mum and I'll come up tomorrow. Thanks!"

6 **only** *einzig* – 7 **Ynys Las** [ˈənəs ˈlɑːs]

Chapter 3

Owain was pleased that James had spoken to him, as he was feeling a bit homesick for Newcastle. It was so far away, and he could not phone his old friends often. He liked trying to speak Welsh, but it was a big effort, so it was good to speak in English after school. Owain was an intelligent boy, and he had noticed that James had problems in the class. He thought a lot about him that evening. "James is sometimes loud, but I think he's a bit worried too," he said to himself. "It's difficult for him in a new country. Perhaps if we make friends it will be easier for both of us. The others in the class already have lots of friends." But Owain did not like the way James sometimes spoke about Welsh. "He is wrong," Owain thought. "I must help him to understand that Welsh is just as important as English here – or maybe more important!"

So next day at three thirty James went to 'Ynys Las' with Owain. Owain's mum, Marged, was in the kitchen.

"Oh, you're back, Owain. And this must be James. How nice to see you. Sit down at the table – I've made something nice for you both."

And with that she put down two glasses of lemonade and a large plate of Welsh cakes. James wasn't sure if he would like the Welsh cakes – he preferred crisps and chocolate when he came home from school. His mother did not bake much, and when she did, the food was often burnt. But Owain was looking very happy as he thanked his mother, so he was sure they must be something special.

2 **to feel homesick** *Heimweh haben* – 5 **effort** ['efət] *Anstrengung, Mühe* – 26 **Welsh cakes** *eine Art Rosinenbrötchen* – 29 **burnt** *verbrannt*

And they were! They were still hot, and they were golden brown.

“Put some butter or sugar on them if you want, James,” said Owain’s mum.

James put sugar on one and ate it. It tasted wonderful! And the lemonade was home-made too. He must ask his mother if she could learn some Welsh recipes. Maybe she could make a fresh start in this new country too.

Chapter 4

As the weeks went by, James began to enjoy classes more. The singing and poetry lessons which were part of the timetable every day were good fun. Everyone in the class was getting ready for the Eisteddfod, which took place in June. Mrs Jones explained to the newcomers that this was a big Welsh festival in which the whole village took part.

"Everybody's good at something," she said. "You can say a poem or tell a story, or you can take part in a play. And, of course, *everyone* can sing!" Mrs Jones was always so enthusiastic.

James also found out about the help which people in Wales were giving to the country of Lesotho, in Southern Africa. His class was saving up for textbooks for a school there, and every week Mrs Evans collected money for this.

"Remember, boys and girls, we're very lucky here in Wales. Everybody has the chance of a good education. Lots of children in Lesotho are too poor to go to school. And those who *do* go need books to study from. So that's why we're saving up for them."

But although he liked these new activities, James still felt that Wales was a strange and new place to him, and he missed Croydon. The other children still laughed at him. They hated his posh accent, and they did not like what he said about Welsh people.

"Sais!" they shouted after him in the playground and in the street. But he now knew this meant 'English', so it wasn't really so awful. Owain tried to

2 **poetry** ['pəʊɪtrɪ] *Dichtung, Gedichte* – 5 **Eisteddfod** [aɪs'teðvɒd] *Kulturfest* – 7 **festival** *Fest* – 11 **enthusiastic** [ɪnˌθuːzɪ'æstɪk] *begeistert*

calm the situation down when he felt things were going too far.
"Stop it, all of you! Just leave James alone!" he said. "He can't help the way he speaks!"
"But you *can* help the *way* you talk to people and the things you say about them, James," he told him when they were alone. "Just think about it. *Why* exactly do you think that people who live here aren't as good as you? And how can you believe that there is only one correct way to speak – *your* way?"
James didn't answer, but he understood what Owain was trying to tell him, and he went very red.

Arwel Jenkins kept on being a bully. Everyone was a bit scared of him, and when he asked for sweets, they always gave him some. But he never bought any himself. He never seemed to have any money at all.
"You're living in our old house!" he shouted at James one day through a large caramel he was eating. "Why did you change its name? It's a tradition here to keep house names. You don't know that because you're not Welsh!"
Arwel's grandfather had owned 'Glanpwllafon' until not long ago. But then he had to sell it because he lost his job, and now the whole Jenkins family lived in a little house in the village. Their new house was much smaller and only had a little garden. They didn't like it at all.
Arwel was lazy at school. He didn't see why he had to work.
"School's boring, and not many people will get a job anyway, so why study?" he always said.

1 **to calm** [kaːm] **down** *beruhigen* – 4 **he can't help sth** *er kann nichts dafür* – 23 **to own** *besitzen*

He didn't always come to class, and then James felt quite glad. Life was quieter then. They were able to do more work when Arwel was not there to make trouble. Mrs Evans was so nice and friendly that all the other pupils wanted to do their best for her.

One Wednesday, however, there was a big fuss. Arwel stood up and shouted all morning, so that it was difficult for the children to do their mathematics. Mrs Evans was helping them, but Arwel kept stopping her and asking stupid questions. When she was finished, he said that the mathematics problems she gave them were too difficult.

"They're not so bad, Arwel. Try some of the easier ones at the top of the page. We'll do the answers together in ten minutes or so. Now, please get on with it – we've got a timetable to follow. And I've got to send our money to Lesotho now."

Mrs Evans was counting the money for Lesotho because it was the end of the month and she had to give it to Mr Phillips. She counted the money in the money-box three times. But it was not as much as the money on the slips of paper in the box. Sadly she decided that some money was missing.

"Boys and girls, there's not as much money in here as there was last week. Can someone tell me if there's been a problem? Has somebody borrowed money for something special?"

"No," answered a group of pupils. They looked serious.

Then Arwel stood up.

"Mrs Evans, it must be James!" he shouted. "He's new. We never lost money before he came. And it can't be Owain – he's been ill at home."

6 **fuss** *Krach, „Theater"* – 15 **to get on with sth** *mit etwas weitermachen* – 22 **slip of paper** *Zettel* – 22 **sadly** *traurig*

James's stomach turned over. He knew that Mrs Evans kept the money in the cupboard, but he had never been near that end of the classroom. All the pupils were staring at him, and he couldn't say a word. He was so shocked.

"Really, Arwel! Don't talk nonsense. That's very silly and not very nice," said Mrs Evans angrily. "Be quiet, and sit down at once. Now, don't listen to him, James. We'll soon find out where the money has gone."

The rest of the day passed by quietly. But James was worried. Did everyone think that he took the money? Did they all believe Arwel? He went home quite upset.

14 **upset** *aufgeregt*

Chapter 5

The following week James met Owain as he went along the street to school. Owain was feeling better now and thinking about all the lessons he had missed. James told him about the theft of the Lesotho money and how Arwel said he had stolen it.
"Mrs Evans said that was stupid, but the class still stare at me sometimes and whisper to each other. And I can't understand all that they're saying."
Before Owain could answer, they saw Arwel in front of them. He was near the village shop and he had two or three packets of sweets in his hand. They walked slowly as they didn't want to speak to him.
"Don't hurry, Owain!" said James. "Arwel will be nasty to me if we meet him."
They let him walk along the street before them.
In the classroom Arwel was quiet that morning – he was too busy eating. When Mrs Evans was not looking, he munched as fast as he could. James thought it was strange that Arwel had so many sweets. Where had he got the money?

The morning went on. The class was practising for the Eisteddfod. They were working on a play in groups. Later on in the year Mrs Evans had to choose the best children to go in for the competition. James was playing a shopkeeper, and a small number of pupils were customers.
When it came to Arwel's turn to speak, all that came out was a lot of munching sounds.

4 **theft** *Diebstahl* – 19 **to munch** *mampfen* – 26 **shopkeeper** *Ladenbesitzer* – 27 **customer** ['kʌstəmə] *Kunde*

"Arwel, please empty your mouth and put the rest of your sweets on my table for the moment. You can't talk with your mouth full."
As Arwel slowly did what Mrs Evans wanted and emptied everything from his pockets, a slip of paper fell to the ground. In one corner of it were the words ELUSEN LESOTHO CHARITY. Total silence fell over the class, and Arwel went red.
"How did *that* get in your pocket, Arwel?" asked the teacher. "I don't know," said the big boy through a mouthful of sweets. "Well, Mr Phillips will want an answer! Go and see him in his office right away."
Arwel went out and shut the door noisily behind him. The class were shocked. But they were also glad that they now knew who had taken their money. James felt better right away. He didn't think anyone really thought that he had stolen the Lesotho money, but it was still worrying him all the time.

When Arwel came back into the classroom, everyone stopped work to look at him. Mr Phillips, the head teacher, was standing at the door. Arwel went straight up to Mrs Evans.
"I'm sorry, Mrs Evans," he said quietly. Then he looked at James. "Sorry, James," he whispered.
"Arwel is going to pay back a little of the Lesotho money from his pocket money every week," explained Mr Phillips. "And he has to write five hundred 'lines' as well. Go and sit down, boy."
Mr Phillips closed the door, and the class went back to their work.

7 **elusen** [e'lɪsen] *(Welsh) Wohltätigkeitsverein* – 7 **charity** ['tʃærətɪ] *Wohltätigkeitsverein, karitative Organisation* – 7 **silence** ['saɪləns] *Stille, Schweigen* – 29 **lines** hier: *Sätze einer Strafarbeit*

Chapter 6

James and Owain knew each other well now and did a lot of things together. They were still the 'new boys', so it was normal for them to be partners. Sometimes James went to visit the Hugheses at 'Ynys Las' after school, and sometimes Owain came to 'Tŷ Ni'. The Boyds did no work on the farm themselves. James's father had his computer job at IBM, and his mother wasn't interested in country life. But they allowed Mr Rees, a local farmer, to use part of their land and to keep his hay in one of their barns. Owain and James liked to watch Mr Rees after school, and sometimes they helped him with the hay.

Mr Rees and the young farm lads who worked for him from time to time were full of fun. They were always laughing as they carried hay from his tractor to the barn. One morning, Mrs Boyd went out into the farmyard to give them all a cup of tea. She was alarmed to see a dirty figure who was coming out of the barn. Hay was hanging from his clothes.
"Don't worry, Mrs Boyd. That's only Siôn. He's been in Llwynon for years. He can help us too," said Mr Rees.
He explained that Siôn was an old tramp who lived in and around the village. He ate old bread from the village shop and soup which friendly farmers or their wives sometimes gave him. No-one knew anything about Siôn.
He had no relatives anywhere. But because he had been there for years, he was part of the local scene,

8 **to be interested** ['ɪntrestɪd] **in sth** *an etwas interessiert sein* – 18 **farmyard** *Hof* – 19 **alarmed** *erschrocken* – 21 **Siôn** [ʃɔːn] – 24 **tramp** *Landstreicher* – 29 **relatives** ['relətɪvz] *Verwandte*

a real character. James and Owain both knew him already, as he often came to 'Ynys Las'. They liked him because he had lots of interesting things to talk about. He told them stories about thieves and bandits in West Wales many centuries ago. Siôn slept all year round in farmers' barns. He spent one or two nights in one farmyard before moving on to another, so nobody minded at all. After all, he could be useful if a farmer needed extra help.

Chapter 7

By the time Easter was near, James was becoming much better at Welsh, although he still felt it was a bit stupid to have to use *two* languages. But Mr Rees the farmer and Siôn, too, spoke mostly Welsh, so he learned quickly. He didn't really notice that as his Welsh got better, he stopped criticising Wales and its language. But the pupils *did* notice, and all the teachers too. James's half-term report said that he was making good progress, especially in Welsh. He felt quite pleased, but he kept quiet about it, of course. So when his Sunday School teacher invited him to sing with his class at the children's church service on Easter Monday morning, he felt brave enough to say yes. Speaking Welsh was difficult, but singing in Welsh was even more difficult! But the regular practice in school for the Eisteddfod was very helpful, and James now knew quite a few Welsh songs and hymns.

Owain's mother, Mrs Hughes, was very enthusiastic about the Easter celebrations in Wales.
"That's one thing they don't have in Newcastle!" she told James when he was at 'Ynys Las' one day in March after school. "And I really missed it. Everyone comes to all the church services, and people who have left Wales years ago come back to their old villages for the celebrations. It's a real family occasion. In Wales it's more important than Christmas!"
"Not many people go to church in England now, do they?" said James.

9 **progress** *Fortschritt(e)* – 12 **church service** *Gottesdienst* – 18 **hymn** [hɪm] *Kirchenlied* – 20 **celebration** [ˌselɪˈbreɪʃn] *Feier* – 27 **occasion** [əˈkeɪʒn] *Ereignis*

"No, they don't. It's the same in Wales. Not many of us go regularly. But Easter is more of a chance to meet people. You see so many old friends. And don't forget, every family has a special lunch on Easter Sunday. Tell your mum she must buy some lamb!"

The Easter weekend went past in the traditional way. Good Friday was a holiday and everything in the village was shut – nobody could buy stamps, sweets or petrol that day. Saturday was also quiet, and Sunday was even quieter. The villagers all went to church in their best clothes. The church service was for the adults, so most of the children did not find it interesting. But they knew that Easter eggs were waiting for them at home after church, and a very special Sunday lunch, so they sat still and kept an eye on the clock.

When James went home, lunch was ready. His mother did not like cooking, but she knew that Easter was important, so she followed tradition. There were three chocolate Easter eggs on the dining room table, and the biggest one was for him. Then the lunch was really great – thick vegetable soup, lamb with roast potatoes, carrots and green beans, followed by ice-cream and trifle. James was very full and very happy.

"That was great, Mum! I can't eat another thing now!" he told his mother.

The next day, Easter Monday, was a more informal celebration at the church. There were three different church services, and people could get food in the church hall, so that they did not have to go home at all. James sat beside Owain at the children's service in the morning.

8 **Good Friday** *Karfreitag* – 24 **roast potatoes** *Kartoffeln, die im Ofen in Fett gebraten werden* – 25 **trifle** ['traɪfl] *eine Art Nachtisch* – 32 **church hall** *Gemeindehaus*

"I don't think it will be too boring," said Owain. "We'll be so busy concentrating on our part in the hymn-singing."

The minister, Mr Roberts, gave a talk which was not too long. He spoke about the help which the people of Llwynon gave to Lesotho. When it was the turn of his class to sing, James could feel the children near him becoming nervous. He got nervous too, and his legs began to shake. But he concentrated completely on the words of their hymn, and soon it was finished. Then he watched Mr Richards, the choirmaster, conducting the rest of the hymns. He was so full of energy that James got worried.

"I hope he doesn't fall off the steps!" he whispered to Owain.

But he didn't, and as the service came to an end, the children were thinking of something very important indeed – lunch.

4 **minister** *evangelischer Pfarrer (in Wales und Schottland)* – 12 **choirmaster** ['kwaɪəˌmɑːstə] *Chorleiter* – 12 **to conduct** *hier: dirigieren*

Chapter 8

After the service Mr Roberts stood at the door saying hello to everyone. Lunch was ready, so they all went to the church hall, where they had hot home-made soup and bread.

James sat at a small table and chatted with the rest of his Sunday School class for a while. He was able to start quite a lot of his sentences in Welsh now, but he usually finished them quickly in English. Nobody really laughed at him any more, and he was slowly adapting to his new life. He felt quite happy. He did not make negative comments about what Welsh people did now or compare them to English people.

Today many people stopped to talk to him as they passed.

"*Sut mae,* James? How are you getting on? Are you enjoying your first Easter here?"

"*Da iawn* – very much." He felt pleased that he could answer in Welsh.

James and Owain helped with the washing-up. They had lots of time before the *Cymanfa Ganu*, the big hymn festival, in the evening.

"This is so different from Croydon," said James. "I didn't do washing-up there. We all played while the grown-ups did the work!" He and Owain chatted as they put the clean plates and cups back on the tables.

At half past six everyone went into the church for the Cymanfa Ganu. The church was full, and the sound of hymn-singing went through the roof. One hymn followed quickly on another, and Mr

5 **to chat** *plaudern* – 16 **sut mae?** [ʃuː maɪ] *(Welsh) wie geht's?* – 18 **da iawn** [dɑːˈjaʊn] *(Welsh) sehr gut* – 21 **Cyrnanfa Ganu** [kɪˈmɑːnvɑː ˈgɑːnɪ] *(Welsh) Tag des Kirchenliedes* – 30 **roof** *Dach*

Richards the choirmaster waved his arms more and more wildly. Everyone really enjoyed themselves. When the hymn festival came to an end, everyone went out into the cold night air. But nobody was in a hurry to go home. People talked to old friends who they only saw on special occasions. James waited with a group of Sunday School friends whose parents were still chatting nearby. Suddenly the sky far away changed from black to orange, and James smelled smoke on the wind. Then he saw flames behind the village – they were coming from the direction of 'Tŷ Ni'!

"Oh dear!" thought James, "I hope that's not *our* house!" But 'Tŷ Ni' was the only house over there behind those trees.

"Dad! Mum!" he shouted. "Look! I think that's *our* house that's on fire – it *must* be!"

James's mother screamed when she saw the flames. She left her friends and hurried along the road home with James. His father and several other men ran down the road as fast as they could.

"Call the fire-brigade – quickly!" someone shouted. What was happening at 'Tŷ Ni'?

1 **to wave** hier: *schwenken, herumfuchteln* – 12 **direction** [dɪˈrekʃn] *Richtung* – 20 **several** *mehrere*

Chapter 9

As Mr Boyd got near to 'Tŷ Ni', the flames sprang higher into the air. He was glad that he knew where his wife and son were. At least the house was empty! Out of breath, the small group reached the farmyard. Smoke was billowing up from it in big black clouds. Then more flames shot up into the air above the barn opposite the house. It was farmer Rees's hay that was on fire! James was both relieved and scared. 'Tŷ Ni' was safe at the moment – but for how long? Someone had phoned for the fire-brigade from the church but they needed twenty minutes to come up the road from Aberaeron.

"The wind's blowing the flames away from the house at the moment," shouted Mr Boyd above the noise of the flames. "Let's hope that it doesn't change direction!"

Some of the men found a hose and tried to put out the fire with water from the kitchen. But the flames were so big that the water was useless. James stayed beside his mother. He felt helpless. What was happening? Why was *their* barn on fire? Was it because they were English? James remembered Arwel's words, "You're not Welsh!" Some Welsh people did not like English families who came to their villages and bought all the houses. Suddenly he had an awful idea. "Arwel wasn't in church this evening," he thought. "Why? What was he doing while they were all singing hymns? Maybe *he* started the fire?"

James knew that Arwel didn't like him. Did he want to get revenge on him? Maybe he thought a small

4 **out of breath** [breθ] *außer Atem* – 5 **to billow** *(her)aufsteigen* – 8 **relieved** *erleichtert* – 13 **to blow** *blasen* – 17 **hose** *Schlauch* – 31 **revenge** [rɪ'vendʒ] *Rache*

fire was fun. But then when the fire had got much bigger, had he panicked and run away? Was Arwel really as stupid as that?

As these ideas went through James's head, the flames sprang higher into the air. Suddenly the bells of the fire engine rang out far away as the fire-brigade came along the little country roads. The noise got louder and louder until the big red machine arrived at the entrance to the farmyard. As the firemen jumped out, James moved behind a tractor to get out of the way. As he did so, he tripped over something which was lying on the ground. The flames lit up a body.

"There's someone here!" shouted James. "Come and help quickly!"

Then, as more flames lit up the sky, he saw that it was Siôn. James got a terrible shock. Poor Siôn did not move at all. His face was black with smoke and he looked completely lifeless.

2 **to panic** *in Panik geraten* – 6 **fire engine** *Feuerwehrauto* – 11 **out of the way** *aus dem Weg* – 16 **to light up** *beleuchten, erhellen*

Chapter 10

One of the firemen ran over to Siôn, while someone phoned for the village doctor and an ambulance. After another fireman put an oxygen mask over his face, he moved a bit and then he groaned.

"Oh, he's still alive. That's wonderful!" thought James. He couldn't say a word because of the shock.

"You're going to be fine, Siôn!" said the fireman calmly.

At that moment Dr Griffiths arrived from the village. The firemen carried Siôn to the farm entrance. A small group of villagers was still standing there. They couldn't fight the force of the fire – it was too strong. Owain was there too, and he looked very worried.

When the ambulance came, Siôn was sitting against a tree. The ambulance team checked him carefully again and laid him on a stretcher. Then they put him into the ambulance, and it drove quickly away to Aberaeron hospital.

The firemen were fighting a terrible battle against the flames. There was fire everywhere, so it was very difficult for them. But after about an hour, most of the flames looked smaller, and the chief of the fire team smiled.

"I think the fire is under control now," he said.

James was relieved. 'Tŷ Ni' was going to be all right. What luck that the wind was weaker now and was not blowing in the direction of the house! Now that the worst was over, he thought of Arwel again. He

3 **oxygen** [ˈɒksɪdʒən] **mask** *Sauerstoffmaske* – 4 **to groan** [grəʊn] *stöhnen* – 5 **to be alive** [əˈlaɪv] *leben* – 11 **entrance** *Eingang, Einfahrt* – 18 **stretcher** *(Trag-)Bahre* – 24 **chief** [tʃiːf] *Leiter*

shouted over to Owain, who was now allowed to come and stand with him.

"Owain, did *you* see Arwel in church this evening? I don't think he was there."

Owain stared at James, as terrible thoughts filled his mind too. "No, he wasn't there – he was only there in the morning and afternoon. You don't think he … ?" Owain's voice went quiet. He could not speak his thoughts to James.

"Well, I think we must try and find out what he has been doing tonight," said James firmly. "But it's all finished for now. And it's too late to do anything tonight anyway. We can ask everyone a few questions in school tomorrow."

6 **mind** hier: *Gedanken* – 11 **firmly** *in entschiedenem Ton*

Chapter 11

Easter Monday was the last day of the school holidays, so it was back to the classroom on Tuesday. The pupils sat quietly at their tables. They were ready to begin their day's work. Mrs Evans told them that the Eisteddfod took place in two months' time. So they must all work hard at the activities that they really liked.

"Everyone's here except Arwel, so you can practise everything you learned before Easter, in groups and alone."

James wanted to ask Mrs Evans why Arwel was not in school. He wanted to know if he was off ill. He hoped that wasn't too nosy.

"Excuse me, Mrs Evans. Will Arwel be here in the afternoon?" he asked politely in Welsh.

Mrs Evans was pleased that James was trying hard to speak his new language. She smiled as she answered him.

"Perhaps he will be. His mother called to say he ate too much at the church yesterday afternoon. So he went home early and was very sick."

So *that's* what happened to Arwel! James was relieved that Arwel was at home when the fire started in the barn. He did not like Arwel, but he didn't think that he was so nasty. There must be another reason for the fire.

The children were practising their poems in the middle of the morning when the door opened and Arwel appeared.

8 **except** *außer* – 21 **to be sick** *sich schlecht fühlen, sich übergeben* – 26 **reason** ['riːzn] *Grund, Ursache*

He still looked quite white. But staying inside at home today was more boring for Arwel than school. And he had something exciting to tell the class.

"My dad's friend's a fireman. He told me that the Boyds' barn burned down last night."

"Don't talk about it, Arwel!" said Owain. "James and his parents got a terrible shock. Keep your mouth shut now."

But Arwel went on talking. "Guess what? I know why the barn went on fire. It was Siôn who started it. He was smoking in the barn and he fell asleep. The fire-brigade found a cigarette end in the hay." Arwel was so pleased – it was not often that he found out things first. "Siôn's still in hospital, but he's feeling better now. And when he comes out he's going to live in an old people's home. But *that's* what's new today – he set the barn on fire!"

"Fine, Arwel," interrupted Mrs Evans. "That's enough. You can finish your story later. Get on with your poems now, please."

After school James went home with Owain at his side. It was busy at 'Tŷ Ni'. Many of the villagers were helping clear away the burned walls, doors and windows of the barn. Others were bringing in tractors full of their own hay to give to Mr Rees. All of his hay was burnt and black. Mr Rees thanked everyone and put the new hay in the tractor shed.

"The tractors can stay outside. The weather's getting warmer now," said the farmer. "It's April, and we won't get any more really cold nights. So the tractors will start easily in the mornings."

Mr Rees and the Boyds were happy, because the neighbours were so helpful to them.

5 **to burn down** *niederbrennen* – 10 **to go on fire** *Feuer fangen* – 11 **to fall asleep** *einschlafen* – 17 **to set sth on fire** *etwas anzünden* – 23 **to clear away** *wegräumen*

"Things will soon get back to normal," said Mr Boyd. "We were very lucky really."

Chapter 12

When it came to June, the children in Llwynon concentrated their efforts on the Eisteddfod. This festival was going to take place in the village hall at the end of the month.

"It is good for you to take part in a public event," Mrs Evans told her class. "And it will help you all too. When you are older you will know how to give a talk in front of a lot of people."

James knew what she meant. For him, speaking or singing in public was an awful experience, but he was getting a bit better every day. He could now stand on the stage and say his poem. But he was still very scared when he had to stand there – he wanted to run away! He and Owain were in the Young Learners' category in the Eisteddfod. He thought of his friends in Croydon – they never said poems or sang in competitions! When he told Owain this, his friend agreed. "Newcastle kids think poems and singing are stupid. If I write to anyone, I won't tell them!"

But here in Wales everyone sang. It was just a part of life.

As Eisteddfod day got nearer, life in the village became more and more hectic. Nobody could avoid the festival activities! Everyone had a rôle to play, even those who did not speak one word of Welsh. James's father, Peter Boyd, had to organise the technical side of things in the village hall, while Mr Rees had to hang the banners high in the street. All the women were baking. Even James's mother could do easy Welsh recipes now, and she said

15 **category** ['kætəgərɪ] *Kategorie, Klasse* – 29 **banner** *Spruchband, Transparent*

she quite enjoyed it. But Mrs Hughes was still the best baker in Llwynon. To James and Owain, the wonderful smell in the kitchen in 'Ynys Las' was a big attraction.

"Can we have some Welsh cakes, please?"

"Well ..." laughed Mrs Hughes. "Let me hear your poem again. If you do it well, you can have some."

The boys both said their Eisteddfod poem really well.

"Well done, Owain," said his mother. "And James, you've got *much* better now. *Da iawn* – very good!"

James was pleased. Mrs Hughes's opinion was important to him.

When Eisteddfod day came, James was very excited. Much to his surprise, he got into the finals of the young Learners' category. And so did Owain.

"You'll do well, Owain, because you've got a good Welsh accent," said James, "but I can't believe how lucky I am!" Then an awful idea came into his head. "But I'll have to stand on stage again, and this time the hall will be full from front to back!" His stomach started to turn over and over.

"Yes, there will be lots of people in the hall," said Owain. "And sometimes the reporter and the photographer from the local newspaper come, too. The Eisteddfod always makes good news."

James tried hard not to get nervous again.

3 **smell** *Duft, Geruch*

Chapter 13

James got up early on Saturday. He wanted to see some of the other competitions before his own turn came. Everyone had to buy a ticket when they arrived at the village hall. They also had to get a special Eisteddfod stamp on the back of their hand. Then you could come and go as you wanted between categories. You just had to show the person at the door the stamp on your hand. The competitions went on all day and a good part of the night.

"Sometimes the last categories aren't over until after midnight," said Mrs Evans. "Some of the judges have a lot to say after each competition."

James was surprised that the judges always said something nice about each person who took part, even the ones who had not done so well. And then they gave the names of the winners in reverse order – third place, then second, and then first. You could feel the tension in the air each time they gave the names of the winners. Then the whole hall clapped and shouted, as the winners smiled happily, while the others tried not to look too unhappy.

The Learners' poetry competition for children between ten and twelve years old was at half past eleven. But the Eisteddfod timetable was already late. This made James more nervous, as they all had to wait longer in the hall. But in the end it was time to compete. There were eight children taking part – James, Owain and six others from different schools. James was the fourth competitor, so he had to wait and listen for his name.

5 **stamp** hier: *Stempel* – 12 **judge** [dʒʌdʒ] *(Preis-)Richter* – 17 **in reverse order** [rɪˈvɜːs] *in umgekehrter Reihenfolge* – 19 **tension** [ˈtenʃn] *Spannung*

"The next competitor is James Boyd – please!"
James walked on to the stage. Everyone in the hall was looking at him as he took his place at the centre of it. He concentrated on his poem and said the difficult words correctly. He couldn't see or hear anything else. Before he knew it, he had reached the end. Then, as he saw all the people, he smiled at them and left the stage.
Owain was next. James didn't look at him – he didn't want to make him nervous. Owain waited for the signal from the chief judge to begin. Then he did the same as James – he concentrated hard on only his poem. He got to the third last line. Then, for some reason or other, he completely forgot the next line! There was total silence in the hall as he stopped. He repeated the third last line, and then went on to finish the poem. As he tried to walk off the stage slowly, he couldn't believe his silly mistake. What bad luck! Today of all days!

All the children knew they had to wait about half an hour before they got the result of the poetry competition. So before the next category began, they left the hall and went into one of the rooms at the back. There were drinks and cakes for them there.
"Never mind, Owain," said James. "The others tripped over some of the words too. And *I* was very nervous! The judges have to remember that we're all just learners."
Owain said nothing, but James could see that he was feeling quite annoyed with himself.
They were enjoying their third or fourth home-made cake when one of the Eisteddfod organisers came in to get them.

"They're judging the poetry now. Hurry!"

James and Owain left their half-eaten cakes and went back to the hall. They just had time to find a seat before the chief judge started on his list of comments.

"We enjoyed all the poems very much. The competitors put a lot of effort into their poems. And you nearly all remembered one thing – it's not just the words of any poem that are important, but how it is presented. Also, the way in which you come on to the stage, stand, and then walk off at the end is very important. The standard of this competition was high, and we found it difficult to choose the winners. However, here they are. Third place, Elinor Davies, Aberaeron School. Second place, Owain Hughes, Llwynon School."

James couldn't stand the tension – but he knew that Owain was better than him.

"First place, James Boyd, Llwynon School. Very good indeed – lots of enthusiasm and a nice Welsh accent. *Da iawn*, James – well done!"

James could not believe his ears. He stood there, unable to think clearly. Someone pushed him forward, and he climbed up the steps to the stage.

"*Da iawn*, James!" repeated the judge.

Everyone cheered and clapped as he hung a small gold medal on a red ribbon round James's neck. As he left the stage, Owain was waiting at the bottom.

"That's great!" he smiled.

"Thanks, Owain – your turn next year!"

"Can we have the winners?" said one of the organisers. "All three of you come outside, please. The photographer's here. He wants to take a photo of you for the newspaper."

1 **to judge** *bewerten, beurteilen* – 10 **to present** [-ˈ-] *darbieten, präsentieren* – 12 **standard** *Niveau* – 24 **forward** [ˈfɔːwəd] *vorwärts, nach vorne* – 26 **to cheer** *jubeln* – 27 **ribbon** *Band* – 27 **neck** *Hals*

The photographer told them to stand near a tree in front of the village hall.
"Now say *cheese*. I need a good picture for the newspaper."
That wasn't difficult! James felt so happy that he was smiling from ear to ear. Fantastic – he was going to get his photo in the paper! That *never* happened in Croydon! For the first time, he felt that he really belonged one hundred per cent in Wales.
"This place is for me," he thought. "I know I'll always like it here now!"

THE END

3 **say "cheese"!** *bitte recht freundlich!* – 9 **to belong** [bɪ'lɒŋ] hier: *sich zuhause fühlen*

Activities

1. Food and drink

Owain's mother bakes, but James's mother does not like cooking. What food and drink can you find here? You must go in a straight line, but you can go in **any** direction*.

S	M	I	L	K	L	J	T	W
T	E	D	A	N	O	M	E	L
I	E	A	M	N	V	L	A	Q
U	F	E	B	X	S	E	P	S
C	F	R	Y	H	E	G	U	P
S	O	B	C	I	Z	G	O	S
I	C	A	R	R	O	T	S	I
B	K	O	T	A	T	O	P	R
E	T	A	L	O	C	O	H	C

PS There are more than 10 hidden words!

* **direction** *Richtung*

2. Word game

How many words can you make? You **must** use the letter in the centre, and you may use the other letters only once.

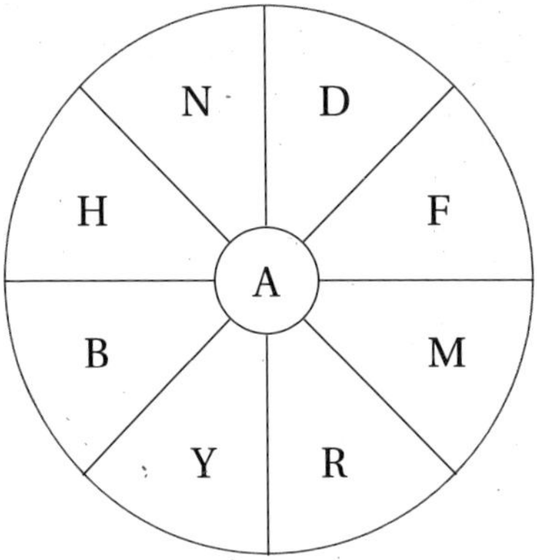

There are many different answers – ask your teacher if you are right!

3. A riddle*

My first is in *cake*, and also in *sweet*.
My next is in *watch*, but not in *meet*.
My third is in *Welsh*, and in *English* too.
My fourth is in *white*, but it isn't in *blue*.
My fifth is in *next to*, and also in *near*.
My whole is a happy time of the year.

What am I?

riddle *Rätsel*

4. Missing words

Can you complete these sentences? If you write down the first letter of each missing word, you will find James's place in the poetry competition.

a) When the Boyds' barn was on fire, the people saw lots of .... from far away.
b) One day Owain did not come to school because he was ....
c) At Easter Welsh people eat lamb with .... potatoes.
d) To .... is to speak loudly.
e) Mr Rees is a farmer, but Siôn is a ....

5. True or false?

a) Arwel has to pay back the charity money he stole.
b) Before Wales, Owain went to school in Newcastle.
c) James's mother is a wonderful baker.
d) Siôn came to Llwynon five years ago.
e) One of the firemen is Arwel's father.
f) James's Sunday School class sings at the church on Easter Monday.
g) Mrs Jones helps children in school who don't speak Welsh.
h) Owain gets third place in the Eisteddfod competition.

6. Meanings

Which answer is right?

a) A *sign* is something that:
  1 gives you information.
  2 makes a loud noise.
  3 lives in the country.
  4 smells good.

b) You make *Welsh cakes* from:
  1 cornflakes.
  2 crisps.
  3 flour.
  4 bread.

c) A *recipe* tells you how to:
  1 sing in church.
  2 get better.
  3 work in the farmyard.
  4 cook or bake.

d) A *customer* is a person who:
  1 cleans and tidies rooms.
  2 buys something in a shop.
  3 works in a shop.
  4 works at an airport.

e) You use *hay* to:
  1 clean the kitchen.
  2 feed farm animals.
  3 put out flames.
  4 take photographs.

f) A *thief* is someone who:
  1 sings in a choir.
  2 bakes cakes.
  3 steals something.
  4 works at the post office.

7. Word groups

Which word does not belong?

a)	1	lamb	d)	1	nasty
	2	egg		2	kind
	3	potato		3	friendly
	4	hay		4	helpful
b)	1	milk-van	e)	1	hymn
	2	tractor		2	song
	3	playground		3	crisps
	4	fire engine		4	poem
c)	1	pullover	f)	1	groan
	2	bag		2	cheer
	3	tie		3	laugh
	4	shirt		4	smile

8. Funny words

Put the letters in the right order and you'll find things you can see or hear at an Eisteddfod:

a) N O S G

d) L A M D E

b) T E A G S

e) M E P O

c) Z P I E R

f) U E G J D

9. Writing

1. The fire in the barn is a terrible accident.
   a) Write a report about it for the local newspaper.
   b) Write a short report of an accident you have heard about.
2. James wins a competition at the Eisteddfod. Write about somebody you know who has won a competition of any kind.

10. Discussion

What new things have you learned about life in Wales from this book?
Go into groups and make a list. Then discuss it all together.

11. Project: Baking Welsh cakes

Here is a recipe for you to try. Translate it first in groups, and then discuss it with your teacher before you start. Good luck with the baking!

Welsh cakes

225 g flour
1 x 15 ml spoon (dessert spoon) baking powder
110 g butter
75 g currants
75 g fine sugar
1 large egg
Half teaspoon cinnamon

To make Welsh cakes you need a heavy frying pan.

First, mix the dry ingredients together, then rub in the butter with your fingers. Then, when the mixture becomes crumbly, add the currants to it. Then beat the egg lightly and add it to the mixture. Mix to a dough, and if the mixture seems too dry, add a little milk. Now roll out the dough to about 5 mm thick. Use a 6.5 c. cutter (or a glass) to cut the dough into rounds. Next, lightly grease the frying pan with cooking fat or margarine. Now heat the pan – not too hot – and cook the Welsh cakes for about 3 minutes each side. They should be cooked through, and they should be quite brown and crisp on the outside. Serve the Welsh cakes warm with lots of butter and home-made jam or honey.

Vocabulary

flour	*Mehl*
baking powder	*Backpulver*
currants	*Korinthen*
cinnamon	*Zimt*
frying pan	*Bratpfanne*
dry	*trocken*
ingredients	*Zutaten*
mixture	*Mischung*
crumbly	*krümelig*
to beat	*schlagen*
lightly	*leicht*
dough	*Teig*
thick	*dick*
cutter	*Ausstechform*
to grease	*einfetten*
cooking fat	*Bratfett*
to heat	*aufheizen*
crisp	*knusprig*
jam	*Marmelade*
honey	*Honig*

Names and places

Arwel ['ɑːrwel]
Ann
Boyd [bɔɪd]
Davies ['deɪvɪs]
Elinor ['elɪnɔːr]
Evans ['evnz]
Gwen
Griffiths
Hughes [hjuːz]
James
Jenkins
Jones
Owain ['əʊɪn]
Marged
Peter
Phillips
Rees
Richards
Roberts
Siôn [ʃɔːn]

Aberaeron [æber'aɪrɒn]
Croydon ['krɔɪdn]
Glanpwllafon [ˌglɑːnpuːhl'ɑːvɒn]
Lesotho [le'səʊtəʊ]
Llwynon [hluː'wɪnɒn]
Newcastle
Tŷ Ni ['tiː 'niː]
Wales
Ynys Las ['ɪnəs 'lɑːs]

Welsh expressions

Bore da ['bɒrə 'dɑː]	good morning
Croeso ['krɔɪsɒ]	welcome
Cymanfa Ganu [kɪ'mɑːnvɑː 'gɑːnɪ]	Hymn Festival
Da iawn [dɑː'jaʊn]	very good
Dosbarth ['dɒsbɑːrθ]	class
Eisteddfod [aɪs'teðvɒd]	Music + Arts & Crafts* Festival
Elusen [e'lɪsen]	charity
Sais [saɪs]	Englishman
Sut mae? [ʃuː maɪ]	how are you?
Ysgol [ə'skɔːl]	school

* arts & crafts *Kunstgewerbe*

Lösungen

1. biscuits, carrots, chocolate, coffee, crisps, egg, lamb, lemonade, milk, potato, soup, tea, Welsh cake

2. far, ran, man, hard, had, day, arm, may, yard, farm, barn, hay

3. Easter

4. **f**lames, **i**ll, **r**oast, **s**hout, **t**ramp = FIRST

5. a) true; b) true; c) false; d) false; e) false; f) true; g) true; h) false.

6. a) 1; b) 3; c) 4; d) 2; e) 2; f) 3

7. a) 4; b) 3; c) 2; d) 1; e) 3; f) 1

8. a) song; b) stage; c) prize; d) medal; e) poem; f) judge